FROM AZUSA TO AFRICA TO THE NATIONS

DENZIL R. MILLER

Second Edition

AIA Publications

The first edition of this book was published in 2005 by Assemblies of God World Missions-Africa Office

All scripture quotations, unless otherwise indicated, are from the HOLY BIBLE, NEW INTERNATIONAL VERSION. Copyright 1973, 1978, 1984, International Bible Society. All rights reserved.

Library of Congress Cataloging-in-Publication Data
Miller, Denzil R., 1946-
From Africa to Azusa to the Nations
Denzil R. Miller

ISBN: 978-0-9903008-3-0

1. History—Church 2. History—Pentecostal. 3. Missions

Printed in the United States of America

AIA Publications
580-D Central Street
Springfield, MO 65802

Website: www.ActsinAfrica.org
E-mail: actsinafrica@agmd.org

CONTENTS

ii

PREFACE TO THE SECOND EDITION

Nothing moves us like a story. Stories have the power to mold our perceptions of reality—of how things are, and of how they ought to be. Possibly more than any other sector of the church, we Pentecostals have embraced the story of the early church as told in the book of Acts. We have made their story our story, their practice our practice, their beliefs our beliefs. Indeed, it was this enthusiastic embracing of the book of Acts that gave rise to the modern Pentecostal movement in the first place.

Yet, Pentecostals have another story, the story of the Azusa Street Revival. They look back to the happenings at 314 Azusa Street in Los Angeles, California, with keen fascination. They take great inspiration from the story. The first edition of this book was published in 2006 during the centennial of that great revival. At the time, I wrote to remind the Africa Assemblies of God (AG), and the larger Pentecostal movement, of its deeply spiritual and missionary roots as exhibited by the workers at the Azusa Street Mission. The book was published in English, French, Portuguese, Spanish, and Chichewa, the language of Malawi where Sandy and I spent fourteen years of our lives as missionaries.

I believed that the story of Azusa Street would capture the hearts of African Pentecostals and inspire them to return to their historic roots—and I was right. The book was well received and widely distributed across the continent. Many testimonies have come our way telling how believers were encouraged and inspired by reading the book. We have receive such comments as, "Now we know who we are," and "We now understand that we have a real history; we are part of something that really matters!"

When the book was first published, significant trends were occurring in the Africa AG. For instance, across the continent the movement was expanding very rapidly. During the decade leading up to turn of the twenty-first century, the church had grown from 2.1 million adherents meeting in 11,800 congregations in 26 countries to 6.3 million adherents meeting in 24,000 congregations in 43 countries, a 200%, 103%, and 65% increase respectively. The trend continued into the new millennium. During the first decade of the century, these advances accelerated, so that, by 2010 the movement boasted 16 million adherents meeting in 65,000 congregations.

At the same time, another important development was occurring in AG churches in Africa. A significant number of local and national churches were beginning to adopt a "we-can-do-it-too" vision of world missions. Across the continent AG churches began mobilizing themselves for aggressive intra-country and international cross-cultural missions. This encouraging trend continues until today.

Regrettably, however, while all of this positive progress was being made, other not-so-encouraging trends were being observed in the church. As the Africa AG was becoming ever larger, it was steadily becoming less and less Pentecostal, at least statistically and experientially. Annual reports from the field revealed that the great majority of AG adherents had not been baptized in the Holy Spirit accompanied by speaking in tongues as described in the book of Acts. Year-by-year the percentage of those baptized in the Holy Spirit was steadily decreasing. In 1993 the annual survey done through the Assemblies of God World Missions, Africa Office, revealed that only 20% of AG adherents in Africa had been baptized in the Holy Spirit. Later, in 2000, another annual report revealed that the percentage had dropped to 17%. The message was clear; this unacceptable trend must be addressed and reversed. If the Africa AG was to maintain its spiritual dynamic and fulfill its missionary calling, the church needed a continent-wide outpouring of the Holy Spirit with millions of its members being empowered by the Spirit.

In addition to this alarming trend, a divergent, spurious form of Pentecostalism was gaining prominence across Africa—and it was beginning to infect AG churches and pastors. Pentecostalism was being redefined from a Spirit-empowered missionary movement that existed to evangelize the lost in the power of the Holy Spirit, to a self-centered movement whose primary mission was to bless and enrich its own members. The gospel of mission was being displaced by a gospel of health, wealth, and personal prosperity. Hordes of self-appointed "apostles" were emerging claiming to be the dispensers of God's blessing— and AG church members were running to them. The movement was in danger of losing its missionary soul. Now, eight years later, the threat remains. At the same time, however, the opportunity for genuine Pentecostal and missional renewal has never been greater.

Another strategic development has occurred in the Africa AG. In March of 2009, three years after this book was first published, the Africa Assemblies of God Alliance (AAGA) unanimously committed itself to a "Decade of Pentecost" beginning on Pentecost Sunday 2010 and continuing through Pentecost Sunday 2020. The Decade of Pentecost is a ten-year, concerted missionary emphasis of the 50 national AG churches in sub-Sahara Africa and the Indian Ocean Basin. At the heart of the emphasis is the goal of seeing 10 million new believers baptized in the Holy Spirit and mobilized as Spirit-empowered witnesses to the lost. Properly harnessed, this powerful spiritual emphasis will inevitably result in thousands of new churches being planted, millions of people coming to Christ, hundreds of new indigenous African missionaries being deployed, and the yet-to-be-reached tribes of sub-Sahara being reached with the gospel. This second edition of the book is dedicated to the success of this bold missionary venture.

This Second Edition contains some minor editorial revisions. It further contains one very significant addition, a new chapter on "The Women of Azusa Street." I added this chapter because I believe the time has come for the women of the Africa AG to assume their God-ordained role as co-laborers with the men in Africa's last-day harvest. Their full participation will be required if the churches are to fulfill their Decade of Pentecost goals of reaching the lost, planting churches, and mobilizing missionaries to the unreached peoples and places of Africa and beyond. In the light of this reality, church leaders are looking again into Scripture, and into their Pentecostal heritage to reevaluate and expand the role women in ministry. I trust that this chapter will help to give historical and scriptural context to that process.

With these things in mind, I commend this Second Edition of *From Azusa to Africa to the Nations* to you. I hope that it will inspire you to embrace the true missionary ethos of authentic Pentecostalism. If you are one of those who has wandered from the missional fold, this book is a call for you to return. If you are one who has remained true to the missionary vision of early Pentecostalism, it is a call for you to recommit yourself to the Pentecostal message of reaching the lost in the power of the Holy Spirit. Whatever your circumstance, it is my hope that you will take inspiration from this book, and that you, with me, will commit yourself to Jesus' final promise to the church:

> *"But you will receive power when the Holy Spirit comes on you; and you will be my witnesses in Jerusalem, and in all Judea and Samaria, and to the ends of the earth" (Acts 1:8).*

Dr. Denzil R. Miller
© 2015

6

INTRODUCTION

An African man once told me, "If you don't know your history, then you don't know who you are." What is true for an individual is also true for a church. The church that does not know its history is free-floating, it has no roots and no clear sense of self identity.

In my contact with Assemblies of God members across Africa I have discovered that the vast majority have no idea about the history of their church or of the greater Pentecostal movement of which it is a part. This book looks back to the common beginnings of both. It retells the story of the glorious revival that God sent to a small mixed-race band of seekers in a rundown out-of-the-way mission in Los Angeles, California, U.S.A., in 1906. The revival has come to be known as the Azusa Street Outpouring. In 2006 the Pentecostal movement celebrated the centennial of that outpouring. It was at Azusa Street that the Pentecostal movement was transformed from a regional religious awakening into a worldwide missionary movement.

This book is an attempt to point the Assemblies of God in Africa back to its Pentecostal and missionary roots. It is my sincere hope that it will serve as a clarion call to the African church to rise up in the power of the Spirit and be all that God has destined it to be.

The Assemblies of God in Africa has in many ways come to a crossroads. Two diverging paths lie ahead. The two paths are represented by two different visions of the gospel. One is the gospel of personal blessing. It says, "Follow Christ and He will give you health, wealth, and prosperity." This message has become the primary message in many of our churches across the continent. The other is a gospel of mission. It says, "Christ died for the sins of all mankind, and He has called us, His Church, to take that message to all nations before He comes again."

The question is, which message represents true Pentecostalism? This book contends that it is the second. It seeks to demonstrate that God raised up the Pentecostal church not primarily for the personal blessing of its members, but to bless the nations in the power of the Spirit. Pentecostalism is essentially a last-days missionary movement.

Even as I write, a great grass-roots missionary movement is emerging in the Assemblies of God in Africa. Across the continent visionary church leaders are boldly calling their churches away from a self-centered "bless me" gospel to a Christ-centered gospel aimed at changing the nations. These leaders believe that what was once called the "dark continent" will soon be a light to the nations. These same leaders know that this can only happen if the African church does two things: First, the church must remain resolutely focused on the mission of God.

Next, it must experience a powerful new continent-wide Pentecostal outpouring with millions of its members being empowered by the Spirit.

It is my hope that this book assists the leadership of Africa in doing both. As you read these pages, I pray that you too will commit yourself to seeking and striving to see that both will come to pass.

10

CHAPTER 1

THE OUTPOURING BEGINS

On the evening of April 9, 1906, an outpouring of the Holy Spirit occurred that would spark one of the greatest missionary movements in the history of the Church. The outpouring happened in an unlikely place, and among an unlikely people. The place was the small four-room home of Richard and Ruth Asberry, located at 214 Bonnie Brae Street in the "colored" section of Los Angeles. Richard was an African-American man who worked as janitor in a local office building. The people upon whom the Spirit was poured out were, in the

▶ The Asberry House, 214 Bonnie Brae Street, where the first outpouring occurred.

words of one writer, "negro wash women, a few of their husbands, and smattering of poor white folks."

The meetings were led by William J. Seymour, a black holiness preacher who had recently arrived in the city from Houston, Texas. He had come to Los Angeles with a message burning in his heart. It was a message of God's grace and power.

Seymour believed that God would give to anyone who would ask, the same experience that He gave to the disciples on the Day of Pentecost, an experience called the baptism in the Holy Spirit. He further believed that those who received this Pentecostal baptism would be given the same "Bible evidence" as the original disciples, they would speak with tongues as the Spirit gave them utterance.

▶ "Irish" Owen Lee received the Holy Spirit when Seymour laid hands on him.

Night after night for several weeks the Bonnie Brae group came together to seek God. However, up until then, none had received the Holy Spirit nor spoken in tongues. Even Seymour himself had not yet received. Determined to succeed in their quest, on April 6 the group committed themselves to a ten day fast, trusting God to answer their prayers.

According to one account, during this time, Seymour was staying in the home of an Irish-American man by the name of "Irish" Owen Lee.[1] On the evening of April 9, as Seymour was leaving Lee's home for the meeting on Bonnie Brae Street, he

---

[1]Robert Owens, "The Azusa Street Revival: The Pentecostal Movement Begins in America" in *The Century of the Holy Spirit: 100 Years of Pentecostal and Charismatic Renewal,* ed. Vinson Synan (Nashville, TN: Thomas Nelson, Inc., 2001), PAGE NOS. Other accounts have Seymour staying at the home of Edward S. Lee who was the first to receive the Spirit in Los Angeles. Others say that it was Lucy Farrow who first laid hands on him.

paused to pray for Lee, who was weak and ill from fasting. Lee then asked Seymour to pray with him to receive the Holy Spirit. As they prayed the Holy Spirit came powerfully upon Lee and he began to speak in tongues.

Filled with excitement Seymour rushed to the Asberry home and told those who had gathered what had just happened. Expectation filled their hearts. Once again, as he had done several times before, Seymour exhorted the seekers from Acts 2:4. He then lifted his hands toward heaven and the Spirit of God came mightily upon him. He was filled with the Spirit and began speaking in tongues. Overcome by God's presence, he fell to the floor, followed by Jennie Moore and then several others. All began speaking in tongues.

News quickly spread, and soon people from all over the neighborhood gathered to see what was happening. Seeing the crowd, and sensing an opportunity to preach the gospel, Seymour and the others set up a makeshift pulpit on the front porch. Seymour then began to exhort the gathering crowd.

In the days that followed the crowds grew larger and larger. One eyewitness reported, "They shouted three days and nights. It was Easter season. The people came from everywhere. By the next morning there was no way of getting near the house. As people came in they would fall under God's power; and the whole city was stirred."[2]

---

[2] Owens, 49.

The meetings at Bonnie Brae continued around the clock. Hundreds were saved, and many were healed and baptized in the Holy Spirit, speaking in tongues just like on the Day of Pentecost. Some witnesses testified that the place literally shook with the power of God. Seymour and the others knew that they had to find a larger building to conduct their services and to continue the revival.

▶ The Azusa Street Mission, 1906

About two miles away was an old dilapidated two-storey wood-framed building. It was situated on Azusa Street, a short dead-ended road in the industrial district of the city. The building was originally used by a Methodist church, later as a warehouse, and finally as a horse stable. It was an asphalt-roofed building 12 meters wide by 16 meters long (40 x 60 feet). It had a flat roof and white weathered clapboard siding. The Gothic arched window above the front entrance was the only feature that identified it as a former church building.

The building was in need of much repair. The doors and windows were broken, and debris was scattered everywhere. In spite of its sorry condition, the building was chosen as the home of the new mission. Volunteers immediately went to work repairing and readying the building for services.

The inside was cleaned and fresh sawdust was spread on the floor. Benches were constructed of empty nail kegs topped by California redwood planks. A pulpit was made from two empty wooden crates and placed in the center of the large lower room with the wood-planked benches arranged in a rectangular pattern around it. The prayer altar was another plank resting on two chairs in the center of the room. The second floor of the building was divided into several rooms. It served two purposes. The larger of the rooms was used as an "upper room" where people could "tarry" to be filled with the Holy Spirit. The other smaller rooms served as living quarters for Seymour and other full-time staff members.

Outside, Azusa Street itself was a dirt road. When it rained people had to wade through the mud to get to the services. The Azusa Street Mission was indeed a humble setting for the great revival that was about to occur.

CHAPTER 2

DAYS OF GOD'S POWER

The new congregation soon moved the revival meetings into the mission at 312 Azusa Street. Their first service was held on April 14, 1906, the day before Easter. From the beginning the services were marked by the presence and power of God. Again

▶ The Azusa Street Mission Committee. William Seymour is seated third from left (front row). Jennie Moore (later Mrs. William Seymour) is third from the left (standing).

and again God showered His blessings on the humble believers who gathered there. Over a three year period thousands were saved, healed, and baptized in the Holy Spirit. From Azusa the message of Pentecost went around the world.

News of the outpouring was spread in various ways. Local newspapers sent reporters to investigate what was happening at the mission. The first news reports appeared in the *Los Angeles Daily Times* on April 18 in an item entitled, "Weird Babble of Tongues." It was a negative report describing the revival in very unflattering terms. Other papers picked up the story and included it in their papers. Although these reports were often negative, they spread the news of the revival far and wide.

In September the Azusa Street Mission began publishing its own paper called *The Apostolic Faith*. The number of subscriptions grew quickly, eventually reaching about 50,000. Very soon the revival grew to be more than a local event: it was quickly becoming a national and international

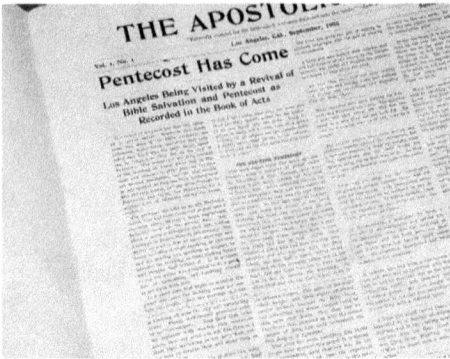

► The First edition of *The Apostolic Faith* announcing that "Pentecost Has Come" to Los Angeles

happening! Within weeks news of the Azusa Street Outpouring was being read all over the United States and in other parts of the world. At the height of the revival, hundreds, and sometimes thousands, of people would attend the meetings, with many crowded around outside the building listening in through the windows.[1]

The banner headline of the first edition of *The Apostolic Faith* boldly announced "PENTECOST HAS COME." The article began, "The power of God now has this city agitated as never before. Pentecost has surely come and with it the Bible evidences are following. Many are being converted and sanctified and filled with the Holy Ghost, speaking in tongues as they did on the day of Pentecost"[2] It further stated that "the real revival is only started as God has been working with His children mostly, getting them through to Pentecost, and laying the foundation for a mighty wave of salvation among the unconverted."

Many wonderful reports came out of the Azusa outpouring. Some witnesses reported seeing a "glow" emanating from the building from several blocks away. Others heard "explosions" that shook the neighborhood. On more than one occasion the Los Angeles Fire Department was called out to extinguish the "blaze" coming from the building.[3]

Day after day the meetings continued, almost without interruption. Sometimes there were as many as nine per day. Services often lasted from early in the morning until late at night. Scores were saved, healed, and filled with the Spirit. According to Robert Owens, "For weeks on end the meetings would blend into

---

[1]Owens, 61.
[2]*The Apostolic Faith*, September 1906, 1.

one another and last twenty-four hours a day. The building was always open, and the meetings started themselves without a leader to initiate them."[4] Owens continues, "The power of God would flow through the room at different times knocking people down.... Often masses of people would simultaneously rush to the altar to seek after God."[5]

Azusa eyewitness Frank Bartleman wrote, "The services ran almost continuously. Seeking souls could be found under the power almost any hour, night and day. The place was never closed nor empty. The people came to meet God. He was always there."[6]

The meetings included spontaneous singing, testimonies, preaching, and "words" from the Lord. Speaking in tongues was often manifested, followed by interpretations. Concerning personal testimonies, Bartleman wrote, "A dozen might be on their feet at one time, trembling under the power of God."[7] Many testified about being drawn to the revival by the Holy Spirit. Some testified of having visions or dreams directing then to Azusa.[8] Two favorite hymns of the revival were "The Comforter Has Come" and "Under the Blood."

---

[3]Owens, 53.

[4]Ibid, 56.

[5]Ibid, 57.

[6]Frank Bartleman, *Azusa Street,* (South Plainfield, NJ: Bridge Publishing, Inc., 1980), 58.

[7]Bartleman, 59.

[8]Owens, 57.

A dominant feature of the revival was the blending of races. People from every strata of society attended the meetings: the educated and the uneducated, the rich and the poor, men and women, native-born Americans and immigrants, locals and foreign visitors. At a time when such a thing was believed to be

scandalous, African-Americans, Asians, Europeans, Hispanics, and whites prayed, sang, and sought the baptism in the Spirit together. Frank Bartleman exulted, "The color line was washed away in the blood."[9]

The lines between clergy and laity were also blurred. Active participation in the meetings was open to all. The people looked to the Holy Spirit to direct the services. Seymour would often sit

► Two favorite songs at Azusa Street: "The Comforter Has Come," and "Under the Blood."

behind his make-shift pulpit with his head inside, interceding for the meeting. When he did preach, he emphasized salvation, personal holiness, divine healing, the second coming of Christ, and the baptism in the Holy Spirit.[10] Personal witness was emphasized: people were encouraged to take the good news to the

---

[9] Bartleman, 54.

[10] Owens, 60.

lost. Seymour admonished, "Now, do not go from this meeting and talk about tongues, try to get people saved."[11]

Many healings took place at Azusa Street. A typical example is the story of a young girl who attended the mission one evening and was baptized in the Holy Spirit. The next morning she went to the meeting and saw a woman who had been crippled for thirty-two years. Prompted by the Holy Spirit, the girl walked up to the woman and said, "Jesus wants to heal you." Hearing these words, the woman's toes and feet straightened out and she began to walk.[12]

Some came to ridicule, but their minds were changed once they came into the atmosphere of the meetings. Some were knocked to the floor by the power of God. Foreigners heard uneducated people praying and speaking in their native languages. One foreign-born reporter was sent to write a negative article on the meetings. However, during the service he heard a woman begin to speak in tongues in his own native language. After the service he approached the woman and asked where she had learned the language of his country. She answered that she had no idea what she was saying when she was speaking in tongues. Although she could only speak English, she had told the

---

[11] Frodsham, Stanley H., *With Signs Following: The Story of the Latter-Day Pentecostal Revival,* Springfield, MO: Gospel Publishing House, 1946, 38, in *The Globalization of Pentecostalism: A Religion Made to Travel,* eds. Murray A. Dempster, Byron D. Klaus and Douglas Petersen (Oxford, UK: Regnum Books International, 1999), 35.
[12] Owens, 58.

man about the details of his sinful life in his own native tongue. Immediately the man renounced his sin and received Christ as his Savior.

Central to the Azusa Street Revival, as with the entire Pentecostal revival, was the message of missions. The Azusa Street participants believed that God was pouring out His Spirit on the church to empower it for worldwide missions before the soon coming of Christ. Azusa helped to birth what is possibly the greatest missionary movement in the history of the Christian church. We will discuss this aspect of the Azusa Street Revival in Chapter 4, "The Global Impact of Azusa."

CHAPTER 3

THE MAN OF AZUSA

As we have seen, the story of Azusa is the story of God's sovereignly fulfilling His purposes in His church. In some ways, however, the story of Azusa is the story of a man, William J. Seymour. Although he was a poor African-American preacher, he was God's chosen vessel to lead the revival. Let's back up for a moment and take a closer look at this man of God.

Seymour was born in Centerville, Louisiana, on May 2, 1870. He grew up in a Baptist home. However, unlike most Baptists, he often had spiritual experiences such as dreams and

▶ William and Jennie (Moore) Seymour, pastors of the Azusa Street Mission.

visions. As a young man he migrated to Indiana where he worked as a waiter in a hotel restaurant. There he joined the Methodist church. He then moved to Cincinnati, Ohio, where joined a holiness group by the name of the Evening Light Saints. This group later became the Church of God, Anderson, Indiana. While in Indiana, Seymour contracted smallpox. The disease left him blind in his left eye.

In 1903, at the age of 33 years, Seymour moved to Houston, Texas. There he met Lucy Farrow, the pastor of a small black Holiness church. In the summer of 1905 Farrow moved to Kansas City, Kansas, to work for Apostolic Faith preacher Charles F. Parham, whom many consider to be the theological father of the Pentecostal movement. In her absence Seymour became the interim pastor of the church. When Farrow returned to Houston the following October, something had changed—*she now spoke in tongues!*[1]

▶ Charles F. Parham set up a short-term Bible Training School in Houston, Texas.

Then, in December of the same year, Parham himself moved to Houston to set up a short-term Bible training school there. In the school Parham taught that the "Bible evidence" of the baptism in the Holy Spirit was speaking in tongues as the Spirit gives utterance.

Seymour wanted to know more about God's word, and he was hungry for more of God. As a result—and with Farrow's strong encouragement—he joined Parham's school. Because of apartheid-type laws in America in those days, Seymour was made to sit outside the room in the hallway by the door. This indignity,

---

[1] You can read more about Lucy Farrow in Chapter 6, "The Women of Azusa Street."

however, did not discourage him. He faithfully attended the classes. As he listened, he came to accept the truth of Parham's teaching concerning the baptism in the Holy Spirit. At this time, however, Seymour did not himself receive the Pentecostal experience.

Soon after this, Seymour received an invitation to hold meetings in a small black holiness church in Los Angeles, California. If things went well, he could possibly become the church's pastor. Feeling that this was the leading of the Lord, Seymour made the 3200 kilometer (2000 mile) trip from Houston to Los Angeles, arriving on February 22, 1905.

Two days later, he began preaching at the Holiness Church on Santa Fe Street. Taking his text from Acts 2:1-4, he preached on the baptism in the Holy Spirit evidenced by speaking in tongues. Because the pastor of the church, Julia W. Hutchins, and some of the other members could not accept this new teaching, they soon locked Seymour and his supporters out of the building.[1]

It was at this time that Seymour and a small group of followers began the prayer meetings on Bonnie Brae Street where the first outpouring occurred, as discussed in Chapter 1. Soon, because of the powerful outpouring of the Spirit that occurred there, and the large crowds that gathered, the meetings were moved to 312 Azusa Street. There, Seymour led the revival for the next three years. During that time this humble African-American

preacher powerfully influenced many others, including such
notables as Gaston B. Cashwell, Charles H. Mason, William
Durham, and John G. Lake. We will talk about these men in the
following chapters.

A Model for African Leaders

William J. Seymour can serve as a powerful role model for
Pentecostal leaders in the African church today. All who knew
him were impressed by his character and humility. Frank
Bartleman described Seymour as "a colored man, very plain,
spiritual, and humble."[2] John G. Lake, a personal friend of
Seymour, said, "I do not believe that any other man in modern
times had a more wonderful deluge of God in his life than God
gave to that dear fellow. . . . God was in him"[3]

Seymour is a man with whom Africans can identify.
Although he was born in America, he was truly a son of Africa.
His ancestors had been carried from Africa to America and sold
as slaves to work in the southern plantations. His mother and
father had themselves been slaves but were freed after the
American Civil War. Being the son of former slaves, he, like many
Africans today, understood the debasing effects of colonialism.
Being poor and black in a racially divided society, he understood

---

[1] You can read more about Julia Hutchins and how she changed her mind about
Seymour in Chapter 6, "The Women of Azusa Street.
[2] Bartleman, 41.

[3] John G. Lake, "Spiritual Hunger," in *John G. Lake: The Complete Collection of
His Life Teachings,* ed. Roberts Liardon (Tulsa, OK: Albury Publishing,
1999), 459.

the indignity of class and racial discrimination. He did not, however, allow these things to shape his life. He rather let God's call on his life shape him.

Throughout his life Seymour was a seeker after God. As a boy his heart was ever open to the influence of the Spirit. As a young man, he sought diligently after God. As an adult he invested his life in doing God's will. And as leader of the Azusa Street Revival, he remained focused, humble, and committed to fulfilling God's will for his life. John G. Lake recalled Seymour's testimony about seeking for the fullness of the Spirit. These are the words of Seymour as Lake remembered them:

> Prior to my meeting with Parham, the Lord had sanctified me from sin, and had led me into a deep life of prayer, assigning five hours out of the twenty-four every day for prayer. This prayer life I continued for three and a half years, when one day as I prayed the Holy Ghost said to me, "There are better things to be had in the spiritual life, but they must be sought out with faith and prayer." This so quickened my soul that I increased my hours of prayer to seven out of twenty-four and continued to pray for two years longer, until the baptism fell on us.[4]

---

[4] John G. Lake, "Origin of *The Apostolic Faith* Movement," in *The Pentecostal Outlook,* September 1932, in Larry Martin, *The Life and Ministry of William J. Seymour* (Joplin, MO: Christian Life Books, 1999), 142-143.

From all descriptions Seymour was a timid man. Yet God used him to lead a great spiritual awakening. What made the difference in his life? I am sure Seymour would credit his success largely to the powerful change that came into his life when he was baptized in the Holy Spirit.

Unlike so many Pentecostal preachers today, Seymour did not present himself as being a great man of God. He rather led the Azusa revival with love and humility. Bartleman wrote that during the services at the Azusa Street Mission "Brother Seymour generally sat behind two empty shoe boxes, one on top of the other. He usually kept his head inside the top one during the meeting, in prayer. There was no pride there."[5] Lake wrote of Seymour's demeanor in the pulpit: "It was not what he said in words, it was what he said from his spirit to my heart that showed me he had more of God in his life than any man I had ever met up to that time. It was God in him that attracted the people."[6]

Except for his strength of character, Seymour could have rejected or compromised the Pentecostal message. He could have allowed pride to keep him from attending the classes of Charles Parham. He could have let discouragement keep from continuing to seek for the baptism in the Holy Spirit. He could have allowed bitterness to keep him from loving and accepting people of other races. And yet he did not allow any of these things to keep Him

---

[5] Bartleman, 58.

[6] John G. Lake, *Adventures in God* (Tulsa, OK: Harrison House Publishers, 1981), 19.

from doing the will of God. Pastor William J. Seymour is a man we can all look to for inspiration.

CHAPTER 4

THE GLOBAL IMPACT OF AZUSA

Azusa Street's greatest contribution was to global missions. Missions was at the very heart of the revival. Seymour and early Pentecostal leaders believed that God was pouring out the "latter rain" to empower the church for worldwide witness. They believed that the primary purpose of the baptism in the Holy Spirit was to empower the church to preach the gospel to all nations before the soon coming of Christ.

► Early Pentecostal missionaries from the U.S. West Coast to China and Japan (1907)

Early leaders like Charles F. Parham and William J. Seymour even believed that those who were baptized in the Holy Spirit would always speak in a known language of the world. They would then be able to supernaturally preach the gospel to that particular people without ever having to study the language. This, they believed, would hasten the preaching of the gospel to all people before Jesus' return.

Although few were actually able to do this, still these early Pentecostals closely connected the experience of Spirit baptism with missions. Empowered by the Spirit, they fanned out from Azusa Street and other Pentecostal centers to many nations of the world. Gary B. McGee has noted that "by 1910, some 185 Pentecostal missionaries had been marshaled over a four year period from the outset of the 1906-1909 Azusa street revival."[1] McGee stated further, from William J. Seymour and Azusa Street Mission "a new missiological paradigm would emerge for the twentieth century."[2]

The Azusa Revival contributed to missions in three distinct ways: First, a number of individuals, after receiving Spirit baptism at Azusa, went directly as missionaries to home and foreign fields where they enthusiastically spread the full gospel message. Secondly, a number of veteran missionaries, upon hearing of the revival, went to Los Angeles to receive their "personal Pentecost." After receiving, they returned to their fields of labor as emissaries of Pentecost. Finally, the Azusa Street Revival indirectly sparked a number of missionary movements when certain Christian leaders visited Azusa and were baptized in the Holy Spirit. These newly-

---

[1] Gary B. McGee, "Missions, Overseas (North American)," *Dictionary of Pentecostal and Charismatic Movements,* eds. Stanley M. Burgess and Gary B. McGee. (Grand Rapids, MI: Regency Reference Library, Zondervan Publishing House, 1988), 612.

[2] Ibid.

empowered leaders in turn influenced the churches and movements they led. Let's look briefly at each of these three missionary "streams" that flowed from Azusa:

Directly From Azusa

Some missionaries went directly from Azusa to the nations. Those from this group first received the Holy Spirit at Azusa. They were then (immediately or subsequently) called into missions, and soon went to the field, often with little or no financial backing. In the very first edition of *The Apostolic Faith* (September, 1906), there were no less than thirteen missionary reports. This was less than six months after the initial outpouring in April. The second edition, one month later, had even more missionary reports than the first.

► A. G. Garr was the first white pastor to receive the Holy Spirit at the Azusa Street Mission on June 14, 1906. He and his wife, Lillian, went out from Azusa to India the same year.

For instance, the first edition reported that "eight missionaries have started to the foreign field since this movement began in Los Angeles a few months ago. About thirty workers have gone out into the field."[3] One typical item reported that "in about an hour and a half, a young man was converted, sanctified,

---

[3] *The Apostolic Faith*, September 1906, 1.

and baptized with the Holy Ghost, and spoke with tongues. He was also healed from consumption, so that when he visited the doctor he pronounced his lungs sound. He has received . . . a call to the foreign field."[4] Another item, found in the second edition, stated that "the Pentecostal Gospel has been spreading . . . On the Pacific coast it has burst out in great power and is being carried from here over the world."[5]

Many, once they were baptized in the Spirit, received a passion and zeal to witness to the lost. Some were inspired to take the gospel to various parts of the U.S. Others were directed to take the gospel to the nations in Pentecostal power. One item in *The Apostolic Faith* tells of a prophetic word that was given in one of the services:

> Many are the prophecies spoken in unknown tongues and many the visions that God is giving concerning His soon coming. The heathen must first receive the gospel. One prophecy given in an unknown tongue was interpreted, "The time is short, and I am going to send out a large number in the Spirit of God to preach the full gospel in the power of the Spirit."[6]

Another item reported, "This is a world-wide revival, the last Pentecostal revival to bring our Jesus. The church is taking her

---

[4] Ibid.

[5] *The Apostolic Faith,* October 1906, 1.

[6] *The Apostolic Faith,* September 1906, 1.

last march to meet her Jesus."[7] Missions was clearly at the heart of the Azusa Street Outpouring.

Visiting Missionaries

A second way the Azusa Street Revival contributed to missions was through its impact on missionaries already in the field. A number of these missionaries, upon hearing about the outpouring of the Spirit in Los Angeles, visited Azusa. Some visited while they were in the States on furlough. Others came from distant lands specifically to receive their "personal Pentecost." Once they received, they returned to their respective fields and proclaimed the Pentecostal message. As a result of their work thousands came to know Christ, received the Pentecostal baptism, and became powerful witnesses themselves.

Azusa chronicler Frank Bartleman compared Los Angeles in 1906 to Jerusalem of the first century, calling it "the American Jerusalem." He wrote, "It seemed that everyone had to go to 'Azusa.' Missionaries were gathered from Africa, India and the islands of the sea. Preachers and workers had crossed the continent, and come from distant islands, with an irresistible drawing to Los Angeles. . . . They had come up for 'Pentecost,' though they little realized it. It was God's call."[8]

He wrote further, "All nations are represented, as at Jerusalem. Thousands are here from all over the Union, and from

---

[7]Ibid., 4.
[8]Bartleman, 53.

many parts of the world, sent of God for 'Pentecost."[9] He then stated prophetically, "These will scatter the fire to the ends of the earth. Missionary zeal is at white heat. . . . The revival will be a world-wide one, without doubt."[10]

Church Leaders

The greatest impact of the revival, however, was not the missionaries that went out directly from Azusa, or even the missionaries who came from afar to be filled with the Spirit, but the indirect impact that the outpouring had on missions movements across the U.S. and around the world. Robert Owens wrote, "Thousands of letters attest that many from around the world eventually received the baptism with the Holy Spirit after merely hearing of the Azusa Street Outpouring and asking God to touch them where they were."[11]

▶ William Durham received the Spirit at Azusa. He became a power influence for missions.

One man influenced by the Azusa Street Revival was William Durham, pastor of North Avenue Mission in Chicago, Illinois. When he saw how some of his friends who had visited Azusa had been dramatically changed, he went to Los Angeles to see for himself. There on March 2, 1907, he too was baptized in

---

[9] Ibid, 64.
[10] Ibid.
[11] Owens, 57.

the Holy Spirit, evidenced by speaking in tongues. He returned to Chicago with new zeal and power. Under his leadership North Avenue Mission became a center for Pentecostal revival in the American Midwest. Many seekers visited the church to hear and to experience Pentecost for themselves. These then returned to their own churches to spread the Pentecostal message.

Among those influenced by Durham was Robert J. Semple, the first husband of famed Pentecostal evangelist Aimee Semple McPherson. He was baptized in the Holy Spirit at North Avenue Mission. Soon after this he and Aimee went as missionaries to China. Tragically, Semple died soon after arriving on the field. Aimee, however, returned to the U.S. and became a powerful evangelist. She later founded the International Church of the Foursquare Gospel (ICFG). The ICFG currently has 36,000 churches in 143 countries around the world.

Two other men who were influenced by Durham were Swedish immigrants to America, Daniel Berg and Gunnar Vingren. After being baptized in the Spirit, Berg and Vingren were directed by the Spirit to go to Para, Brazil. After being commissioned and sent out from the North Avenue Mission, they arrived in Brazil in 1910 where they founded the Assemblies of God of Brazil, which now numbers over 19 million members. The Brazilian church is now sending its own missionaries to the nations. Berg and Vingren have been called the fathers of the Pentecostal movement in Brazil.

Another influential leader who received the Holy Spirit at Azusa was Charles H. Mason, founder of the Church of God in Christ (COGIC). The COGIC is a predominantly African-American Pentecostal Church in the U.S. Mason visited Azusa in 1907 where he was powerfully baptized in the Spirit. He told of his experience in his own words:

> The first day in the meeting I sat to myself, away from those that went with me. I began to thank God in my heart for all things, for when I heard some speak in tongues, I knew it was right though I did not understand it. . . . I also thank God for Elder Seymour who came and preached a wonderful sermon. His words were sweet and powerful and it seems that I hear them now while writing. When he closed his sermon, he said, "All of those that want to be sanctified or baptized with the Holy Ghost, go to the upper room, and all those that want to be justified, come to the altar.". . . I said that is the place for me . . . Then, I began to ask for the baptism of the Holy Ghost . . . When I opened my mouth to say "Glory," a flame touched my tongue which ran down me. My language changed and no word could I speak in my own tongue. Oh! I was filled with the Glory of the Lord. My soul was then satisfied.

▶ Charles H. Mason received the Holy Spirit at Azusa Street. He led the Church of God in Christ into Pentecost.

Upon receiving the Spirit, Mason returned to his church in Memphis, Tennessee, where he preached the message of Pentecost. Some accepted the message, others rejected it. As a result, the holiness denomination split into two groups. One remained in the holiness camp. Mason's group, however, reorganized as a Pentecostal church. Owens writes that Mason became "a conduit for the fire of the Azusa Street Revival to reach all parts of the United States."[12] The COGIC is now the largest Pentecostal church in the U.S. with 6 million members.

▶ Gaston B. Cashwell was baptized in the Holy Spirit at Azusa. He became the "Apostle of Pentecost to the South,"

Another early Pentecostal leader who received the Spirit at Azusa Street was Gaston B. Cashwell. Cashwell was a leader in the Holiness Church in North Carolina. Like Mason, when Cashwell visited Azusa, he was at first repulsed by the noise. He was also disturbed by the interracial mixing he saw at the mission. God, however, convicted him of his racial prejudice. He humbled himself and received the Spirit when several young African-American boys prayed with him. He then returned to North Carolina and led his church into Pentecost, changing its name to the International Pentecostal Holiness Church (IPHC). He was mightily used by God to spread the Pentecostal message

---

[12] Ibid., 66

throughout the southern U.S. and became known as the "Apostle of Pentecost to the South." Today the IPHC has 1.6 million members worldwide. Cashwell also influenced the Church of God (Cleveland, TN) to join the ranks of Pentecost. The Church of God is the oldest Pentecostal denomination in America. It now has over 26,000 churches in 164 countries with a membership of 5.8 million people.

Thomas Ball Barratt of Norway is known as the Pentecostal apostle to northern and western Europe. He was also influenced by the Azusa Street Revival. Barratt was an English immigrant to Norway where he was ordained an elder in the Methodist church. In 1906 he

▶ Thomas Ball Barratt was filled with the Spirit after reading *The Apostolic Faith*. He became the Pentecostal apostle to northern and western Europe.

made a fund raising trip to the U.S. While in New York City he read reports of the Azusa Street Revival in *The Apostolic Faith*. He then wrote to the Azusa Mission asking how he could receive the Spirit. They wrote him back telling him to seek for the Spirit daily. He followed their advice and was soon powerfully baptized in the Holy Spirit. He then returned to Oslo full of zeal and spiritual power. There in December, 1906, he conducted the first Pentecostal services in Europe. He later traveled to Sweden, England, France, and Germany, where he sparked other national Pentecostal movements. Barrett was used by God to bring into the

movement such leaders as Lewi Pethrus in Sweden, Jonathan Paul in Germany, and Alexander Boddy in England.

Many founders and early leaders of Assemblies of God were influenced by the Azusa Street Revival. Ernest S. Williams was baptized in the Spirit at the Azusa Street Mission. J. Roswell Flower was influenced by William Durham.

CHAPTER 5

AZUSA AND AFRICA

Missionaries went out from the Azusa Street Mission to many parts of the world, including the United States, Canada, Northern Europe, Western Europe, and China. Africa, however, seems to have been a primary focus of the mission. *The Apostolic Faith* reports on visitors from Sudan,[1] Ethiopia,[2] and Cape Verde Islands[3] attending the meetings. Gary B. McGee writes, "Advances into Africa targeted Liberia and Portuguese Angola with a team from Azusa Street that included several African Americans. To Liberia went the G. W. Batmans, Julia W. Hutchins, and Lucy Farrow. The veteran Methodist missionaries Samuel and Ardella Mead traveled with the Robert Shidelers to Angola."[4]

Below is a list of some of the missionaries that are reported on in *The Apostolic Faith* newspaper. All were baptized in the Spirit at Azusa, except Lucy Farrow, who came to Los Angeles

---

[1] *The Apostolic Faith,* September 1906, 1.

[2] Ibid., 3.

[3] Ibid., 1. You can read more about Julia Hutchins and Lucy Farrow in Chapter 6, "The Women of Azusa Street."

[4] Gary B. McGee, "To the Regions Beyond: The Global Expansion of Pentecostalism," in *The Century of the Holy Spirit: 100 Years of Pentecostal and Charismatic Renewal,* ed. Vinson Synan (Nashville, TN: Thomas Nelson, Inc., 2001), 88.

from Houston already full of the Spirit. All went out from Azusa to Africa as pioneer Pentecostal missionaries.

From Azusa to Africa

S. J. and Ardella K. Mead were already veteran missionaries to Central Africa before visiting Azusa. Sensing a lack of power in their lives and ministries, they made their way to the mission in August or September of 1906 to receive the fullness of God's Spirit.[5] About two or three months later, in the November edition of *The Apostolic Faith* a report reads, "Our dear Brother and Sister Mead, who have spent twenty years in missionary work in Africa have received their Pentecost in Los Angeles, and as the Lord leads and opens the way they will be on their way to the dark continent again with divine fitness for missionary work."[6] The Meads later left for Africa with a group from the mission. The paper reported,

> Workers are constantly going out trusting God for their support. A Band of six missionaries left for Africa. They are Bro. and Sister S. J. Mead, Bro. and Sister Robert Shideler, and Bro. and Sister G. W. Batman. . . . They are going to two points in Africa. God bless them and make them a great blessing. We must keep them on our hearts in prayer for they are our brothers and sisters. . . . The Lord is sending revivals everywhere that workers have gone that are baptized with the Holy Ghost and fire.

---

[5]*The Apostolic Faith,* September 1906, 3.

[6]*The Apostolic Faith,* November 1906, 3.

Many more are being fitted up and called for the field, for the fields are white ready for the harvest.[7]

Another article concerning the G. W. Batmans reads that they were "all packed up for Monrovia, Liberia, Africa. They have three little children, but are willing to trust the Lord." The report said that Batman had been given a vision of a town on the west coast of Africa where they should go.[8]

Thomas P. Mahler also went out as a missionary from Azusa to Africa. As he was leaving for the field, a message in tongues and interpretation was spoken over him, saying, "I have anointed this dear one with my Spirit, and he is a chosen vessel to me to preach the gospel to many, and to suffer martyrdom in Africa."[9] We don't know if that prophecy was ever fulfilled.

Surprisingly, Julia W. Hutchins also went from the Azusa mission as a missionary to Liberia, West Africa. Remember, Hutchins was the pastor who locked Seymour out of the Holiness Church on Santa Fe Street when he first came to Los Angeles. She obviously, at some point, had a change of heart. And Seymour, the gracious man that he was, must have forgiven her. Her testimony appears in *The Apostolic Faith*. She writes, "I am ready and down to the Mission with my ticket and everything prepared, waiting to have hands laid on and the prayers of the saints, and

---

[7] Ibid., 4.

[8] Ibid., 2, ref. p. 3.

[9] *The Apostolic Faith*, September 1906, 4.

expect to leave at eight o'clock from the Santa Fe station en route for Africa. We expect to go to Mt. Coffee, Monrovia, Liberia."[10]

Another article is the testimony of a young lady by the name of Leila McKinney. She spoke of her call to Africa, and how God had made provision for her fare. She wrote, "I am willing to trust Him through to Africa. I know the Lord wants me to go there. I want to testify to the people and teach the children about the blessed Lord, and to work for the Lord. I am willing to forsake all my loved ones for His sake."[11]

Finally, Lucy Farrow, the first person to tell Seymour about the baptism in the Holy Spirit and speaking in tongues, also went as a missionary to Liberia. A brief report in *The Apostolic Faith* tells of her journey to Africa via New York City: "Sister Lucy Farrow wrote from New York that she had started for Africa. About two hundred souls had been saved in Portsmouth and most of them are speaking in tongues. She sends love to the saints and asks for your prayers."[12]

John G. Lake

The most well-known, and certainly the most successful Africa missionary connected to the Azusa Street Mission, was John G. Lake. Although Lake had been baptized in the Holy Spirit

---

[10] Ibid., 1. (You can read more about Julia Hutchins in Chapter 6, "The Women of Azusa Street.")

[11] *The Apostolic Faith,* October 1906, 1.

[12] Ibid., 3.

before visiting Azusa, he did visit the mission, and became a personal friend of William Seymour.

Lake began his ministry as a Methodist preacher. He received the Pentecostal experience and spoke in tongues under the ministry of Charles Parham in Zion, Illinois, in 1907. After being baptized in the Holy Spirit, Lake answered a long-standing call to minister in South Africa. In April 1908, he led a missionary party to Johannesburg, where he began to spread the Pentecostal message throughout the nation. With him were his wife and seven children as well as Thomas Hezmalhalch and J. C. Lehman.

▶ John G. Lake went as a missionary to South Africa.

Lake was mightily used of God in South Africa in preaching the gospel with supernatural signs following. He succeeded in founding two large and influential Pentecostal churches. The white branch took the name "Apostolic Faith Mission," borrowing its name from the famous mission on Azusa Street. The black branch eventually developed into the Zion Christian Church. Sadly, this church adopted many non-biblical doctrines and practices. It is the largest church in South Africa. According to Gordon Lindsay, at the end of his five years in South Africa Lake's missionary work had resulted in 1,250 preachers, 625 congregations, and 100,000 converts.[13]

South African empire builder Cecil Rhodes said about Lake, "His message has swept Africa. He has done more toward South Africa's future peace than any other man." The Indian leader Mahatma Ghandi said of Lake, "Dr. Lake's teachings will eventually be accepted by the entire world." Both John G. Lake and the other Azusa Street missionaries made significant contributions to the spread of the light of the gospel in Africa. The Pentecostal church in Africa shares a close affinity to the gospel mission once located at 312 Azusa Street.

▶ **Front Row:** John G. Lake with William Seymour at the Azusa Street Mission. **Back Row:** Brother Adams, F.F. Bosworth, and Tom Hezmalhalch.

---

[13] Gordon Lindsay, ed., *John G. Lake: Apostle to Africa* (Dallas, TX: Christ for the Nations, 1979), 53.

CHAPTER 6

THE WOMEN OF AZUSA STREET

One cannot adequately tell the story of Azusa Street without talking about the women who so valuably contributed to the work. It fact, without these women there would have been no Azusa Street revival, at least not in the way it happened.

Five years before the Los Angeles outpouring, Pentecostal historians trace the beginning of the modern Pentecostal Movement back to Topeka, Kansas, where on January 1, 1901, a humble holiness woman named Agnes Ozman was the first to be filled with the Spirit and began speaking in tongues as the Spirit gave utterance. This occurred at Charles Parham's Bethel Bible School. Just as in the book of Acts, the Spirit opened the heart of a woman to be the first person to receive the gospel in Europe

► Agnes Ozman was the first to receive the Spirit in the Topeka Revival

(Acts 16:14), in Topeka the Spirit opened the heart of a woman to be the first to receive the Spirit in the modern Pentecostal revival.

At Azusa Street many women of various ethnic backgrounds were filled with the Spirit and empowered to teach, preach, and plant churches. They also went as Pentecostal emissaries to cities throughout the U.S.A. and to various parts of the world, including Africa. Along with the men, these anointed women gave spiritual and administrative oversight to the work. In fact, six of the twelve administrative elders at Azusa Street were women. As such they were entrusted with the duty of ordaining evangelists, planting churches, and sending out missionaries from the mission to spread the good news that "Pentecost has come."[16] Estrelda Alexander has noted,

> At a time when the larger society was still wrestling with the issue of a woman's rightful place, these women found a place for themselves at Azusa Street. While most denominations had not begun to ordain women or allow them in the pulpit, these women claimed for themselves ordination by God and made a pulpit wherever they found themselves at the Azusa Street Mission and on the surrounding streets and campgrounds.[17]

These Pentecostal women believed that the Spirit Himself had qualified them and dispatched them to preach the gospel. They based this belief on Jesus' promise of Acts 1:8 and on Joel's promise in 2:28-29 which Peter quoted on the Day of Pentecost.

---

[16] "Pentecost Has Come" was the headline on the first edition of *The Apostolic Faith* newspaper published by the Azusa Street Mission in September 1906. The subhead proclaimed, "Los Angeles is Being Visited by a Revival of Bible Salvation and Pentecost as Recorded in the Book of Acts."

[17] Estrelda Alexander, *The Women of Azusa Street* (Laurel, MD: The Seymour Press), 38.

They often cited Paul's admonition that in Christ "there is neither Jew nor Greek, slave nor free, male nor female, for you are all one in Christ Jesus" (Gal. 3:8). They interpreted Paul's prohibitions concerning women teaching and preaching in 1 Corinthians 14:35 and 1 Timothy 2:11-14 as dealing with local situations. However, Joel's promise that "your sons *and your daughters* shall prophesy" they saw as a universal principle to be believed and acted upon during these last days of time when God was pouring out His Spirit on "all flesh." This chapter will feature four of these remarkable women of Azusa Street.

Julia Hutchins

Julia Hutchins holds a special place in the history of the Azusa Street revival, for she was the African-American pastor who invited William Seymour to come from Houston to Los Angeles to serve as pastor of the Santa Fe Street Holiness Mission. As you will remember from Chapter 1, it was she who locked Seymour out of the church because of his teaching on the baptism in the Holy Spirit. Thankfully, however, her story does not end there. She soon repented of this action and became a whole-hearted supporter of Seymour and his teaching that tongues is the "Bible evidence" of one's being baptized in the Holy Spirit.

At the Azusa Street Mission Hutchins was herself baptized in the Holy Spirit and reaffirmed an earlier call to go to Africa as a missionary. Within five months of the beginning of the revival she and her husband, along with their young niece, Leila McKinney, left the mission to go as missionaries to Liberia on the

West African coast. They were accompanied by G. W. and Daisy
Batman, and Lucy Farrow.

Upon leaving Azusa Street Hutchins and her colleagues
preached their way across the heartland of America to the East
Coast. From there they proceeded by ship to Liverpool, England.
From Liverpool they sailed to Monrovia, Liberia. All along the
way the missionaries faithfully spread the message of Pentecost.
One report posted in *The Apostolic Faith* reads, "Sister Hutchins
has been preaching the Gospel in the power of the Spirit."[18] We
know little of Julia's ministry in Liberia nor how long she stayed;
however, we do know that she was one of the first Pentecostal
missionaries to set foot on the African continent. Like many early
Pentecostal women, her story simply fades into history. We can
assume that when Julia returned to the U.S.A. she continued to
minister in the Spirit until her death.

Lucy Farrow

Of all the women of Azusa Street, Lucy Farrow is arguably the
most notable. It was she who first introduced William Seymour to
Charles Parham and to the Pentecostal experience. While we have
already mentioned her in a previous chapter, more needs to be
said about this extraordinary woman. She was reportedly the
niece of the famed American abolitionist and friend of Abraham
Lincoln, Fredrick Douglass. Although Lucy Farrow was born into

---

[18] "Testimonies of Outgoing Missionaries." *The Apostolic Faith,* Vol. I, No. 2,
(October 1906).

slavery, by the time she met Seymour in 1905 she was serving as pastor of a small Afro-American Holiness church in Houston, Texas. As you will remember from Chapter 3, Farrow encouraged Seymour to attend Parham's Bible school where he was convinced concerning Parham's view of the baptism in the Holy Spirit.

Lucy Farrow has been called "the central prophet igniting the Holy Ghost fires in Southern California."[19] She was known for her success in praying with people to receive the gift of the Holy Spirit. Even before the first outpouring on Bonnie Brae Street, Seymour sent for Farrow to come to Los Angeles and help him pray with seekers. Once in the city she was responsible for leading many at the Azusa Street Mission into the baptism in the Holy Spirit. According to Frank Ewart, "Within a few days of her arrival, the revival broke out in earnest and one person after another began receiving the Pentecostal experience..."[20] Some even say that it was she and not Seymour who prayed with Irish Owen Lee to receive the Holy Spirit thus igniting the Bonnie Brae Outpouring that led to Azusa Street.[21]

A mature minister of the gospel, Farrow became a key figure in the Azusa Street revival. She was admired for her wise spiritual

---

[19] Alexander, 39.

[20] Frank Ewart, *The Phenomenon of Pentecost* (Hazelwood, MO: World Aflame Press, 1947), 74-76, in Estrelda Alexander, *The Women of Azusa Street*, 42.

[21] Roberts Liardon, *The Azusa Revival*, (Shippensburg, PA: Destin Image Publishers, 2006), 159-160.

leadership and often taught and preached alongside Seymour. She also served on the mission's administrative board.

In addition to her work in Los Angeles, Farrow conducted preaching tours in Texas, Louisiana, North Carolina, Virginia, and New York. During one meeting in Texas in August of 1906 Farrow convinced Howard Goss concerning the truth of the doctrine and personally lead him into the experience of Spirit baptism. Goss was a key figure in the early Pentecostal movement and would become one of the founders of the Assemblies of God. He testified, "I went forward that she might place here hands upon me. When she did, the Spirit of God again struck me like a bolt of lightning; the power of God surged through my body, and I began speaking in tongues."[22] Along with the Julia Hutchins family and the G. W. Batmans, she was among the first Pentecostal missionaries to go to Africa.

During her seven months in Africa, Farrow lived and ministered in Johnsonville, Liberia, about 25 miles east of Monrovia.[23] During one revival in Liberia in a report to *The Apostolic Faith* dated March 26, 1907, the team wrote,

> We opened a ten days' meeting in a school house, and on the tenth night, the Lord came in mighty power. Two were baptized with the Holy Ghost and spoke in tongues. Ten here have received sanctification, and five are filled

---

[22] Ethel Goss, *Winds of God* (New York: Cornet Press Books, 1958), 56, in Estrelda Alexander, *The Women of Azusa Street,* 44.

[23] *The Apostolic Faith,* Vol. I. No. 11, (October-January, 1908).

with the Holy Ghost and speaking in tongues. A brother and his household have been baptized with the Holy Ghost. God has called him to the ministry…[24]

When she returned to the U.S. Farrow lived with her son and his wife in Houston, Texas, for five years where she continued to lead believers into the baptism in the Holy Spirit. In 1911, only five years from the beginning of the Azusa Street revival, she died of intestinal tuberculosis at the age of sixty years. As with many other women of Azusa Street, her contribution and to the emerging Pentecostal movement was immense.

Jennie Seymour

Jennie Evans Moore Seymour has been called "perhaps the most influential woman in the life and ministry of William Joseph Seymour."[25] She was one of seven people who received the Spirit and began to speak in tongues during the initial outpouring on Bonnie Brae Street. With her speaking in tongues, however, came another miracle. Robert Owens writes,

► Jennie Seymour became a leader in the Azusa Street Revival

She began to play beautiful music on an old upright piano, and to sing in what people said was Hebrew. Up until this time she had never played the piano, and although she never

---

[24] *The Apostolic Faith*, Vol. 1, No. 7, (April 1907), 1.

[25] Alexander, 151.

took a lesson, she was able to play the instrument for the rest of her life.[26]

Here is her own testimony as recorded in *The Apostolic Faith* newspaper:

> On April 9, 1906, I was praising the Lord from the depths of my heart at home, and when the evening came and we attended the meeting the power of God fell and I was baptized in the Holy Ghost and fire, with the evidence of speaking in tongues.... I sang under the power of the Spirit in many languages, the interpretation both words and music which I had never before heard, and in the home where the meeting was being held, the Spirit led me to the piano, where I played and sang under inspiration, although I had not learned to play.[27]

Two year later in May of 1908 she became the wife of William J. Seymour.

Jennie was one of the mission's "city evangelists" and was known for her powerful preaching and beautiful singing. She, along with others, made at least one trip to Chicago to William Durham's North Avenue Mission. She wrote from Chicago, "Truly, beloved, the mission at 943 W. North Avenue is a blessed

---

[26] Robert Owens, "The Azusa Street Revival: The Pentecostal Movement Begins in America," *The Century of the Holy Spirit: 100 Years of Pentecostal and Charismatic Renewal,* Vinson Synan, ed. (Nashville, TN: Thomas Nelson, Inc., 2001), 48.

[27] *The Apostolic Faith*, Vol I, No. 8, May 1907.

place—many Spirit-filled men and women and children. They have more children than at Azusa and they are filled. Beloved, I would you could see them."[28]

During the years following the revival she became co-pastor of the Azusa Street Mission along with her husband, William. At his death she assumed leadership of the church. In 1907, remembering the day when she was first baptized in the Holy Spirit, Jennie wrote, "God is continuing to use me to His glory ever since that wonderful day, and I praise Him for the privilege of being a witness for Him under the Holy Ghost's power."[29]

Rachel Sizelove

Rachel Harper Sizelove holds a unique place in the Azusa Street revival and in the early history of the Pentecostal Movement. She is noted, not so much for what she did at Azusa Street, but for carrying the message of Pentecost from Azusa to Springfield, Missouri, the future home of the General Council of the Assemblies of God.[30]

► Rachel Sizelove carried the message of Azusa Street to Springfield, Missouri

---

[28] *The Apostolic Faith,* Vol. I. No. 12, (January 1908).

[29] *The Apostolic Faith* Vol. I, No. 8, (May 1907).

[30] Much of the material in this section is taken from Estrelda Alexander, "Chapter 19: Rachel Harper Sizelove," *The Women of Azusa, Street* (Laurel, MD: The Seymour Press), 166-176.

When Rachel and her husband, Josie, arrived in Los Angeles in 1895, they had been holiness circuit-riding evangelists for more than twenty years. They began attending the Azusa Street meetings in June of 1906, just two months after the revival began. Rachel told of their first visit to the mission: "As we entered the old building, somehow, I was touched by the presence of God."[31] Within a month both she and Josie had been baptized in the Holy Spirit and spoke in tongues.

Rachel was later licensed to preach by the Azusa Street Mission. There is, however, no record of any major role she played in the mission. Her greatest contribution to the revival is the fact that in May of 1907 she carried the message of Azusa to Springfield, Missouri. She wrote of her calling to Springfield: "The Lord showed me that I must go back east and tell my mother and brothers and sisters what the Lord had done for me and bring them the blessed message."[32]

When she arrived in Springfield, Rachel began a cottage prayer meeting in her family's living room. In these home meetings several were filled with the Spirit, including her sister, Lillian Corum, and other family members. As the excitement mounted, Rachel and some volunteers from Joplin purchased a large tent where they held gospel meetings for several weeks. At times the meeting drew large crowds.

---

[31]Rachel Sizelove, "A Sketch of My Life," unpublished manuscript, 196.

[32]Rachel Sizelove, "A Sparkling Fountain for the Whole Earth," *Word and Work*, Vol. 56, No. 6 (June 1934), 2.

Sometime in 1907 Rachel returned to Los Angeles, stayed for a while, and with her husband, Josie, returned to Springfield. For several months the couple travelled throughout the region preaching the gospel and proclaiming the message of Pentecost. It was during this time that she had her famous "sparkling fountain" vision. She wrote about this vision in an article for the *Word and Work* magazine entitled, "A Sparkling Fountain for the Whole Earth":

> There appeared before me a beautiful, bubbling, sparkling fountain in the heart of the city of Springfield. It sprang up gradually but irresistibly and began to flow toward the East and toward the West, toward the North and toward the South, until the whole land was covered with water.[33]

Rachel's vision proved to be prophetic, for it was on that very spot that in November of 1913 she and her sister, Lillian, began a church that was to become Central Assembly of God, the "mother church of the Assemblies of God." One year later in April of 1914 in Hot Springs, Arkansas, the Assemblies of God was founded. Seven years later in 1922 Central Bible College, the denomination's first ministerial training school, was begun in the church's basement. Soon a publishing house was added. In 1918 the Assemblies of God moved its headquarters to Springfield where it remains until today.

---

[33]Sizelove, "Sparkling Fountain," 2.

Possibly more than any other church, the Assemblies of God owes its existence to the Azusa Street revival, for it was from churches birthed during that revival that the denomination was primarily formed. Today the Assemblies of God has become the largest Pentecostal church in the world with more than 366 thousand churches and 67 million constituents worldwide.[34] It has truly become, in the words of Rachel Sizelove, a "sparkling fountain for the whole world."

Julia Hutchins, Lucy Farrow, Jennie Seymour, and Rachel Sizelove are but four of many women who significantly participated in the Azusa Street revival. They and thousands of other unnamed women have powerfully contributed to the spread of Pentecostalism throughout the world. The Pentecostal church is deeply indebted to these courageous women. They have truly helped to make the movement what it is today.

Today God's Spirit is moving across Africa as never before. The Africa Assemblies of God has launched a "Decade of Pentecost" from 2010 to 2020 with the goal of seeing 10 million men and women baptized in the Holy Spirit and mobilized as Spirit-empowered witnesses, church planters, and missionaries to the unreached peoples and places of Africa.[35] As never before God is calling on the women of Africa to take their rightful place in the work of harvesting the lost before Jesus' soon return.

---

[34]Assemblies of God, 2013 statistical report.

[35]Decade of Pentecost website: www.DecadeofPentecost.org.

African Pentecostal women can take great inspiration from the noble women of Azusa Street, and they can follow their example. They too can seek God, be empowered by His Spirit, and then go out in the Spirit's power to tell others the good news of Christ.

CHAPTER 7

THE MESSAGE OF AZUSA

As we near the end of our study and think about the great outpouring of the Spirit at Azusa Street, we ask an important question: What is the message of the Azusa Street Revival for the African church today? While many lessons can be learned, four are particularly pertinent:

God Can Use Anyone

The first lesson we learn is that God can mightily use anyone who will commit himself or herself fully to His purposes. It does not matter to God what cultural or economic background the person may be from, or how marginalized or poverty-ridden his society may be—God can use any person from any background to impact the world with the gospel, if only that person will consecrate himself or herself fully to God's mission and be genuinely empowered by the Holy Spirit.

The participants in the Azusa Street Revival were not from the wealthy or privileged class of society. They were mostly from the poorer working class. And yet, they discovered a great truth, the truth of God's empowering presence. This truth, and the experience it revealed, freed them to be all that God wanted them to be. Thus liberated, they were willing to give all for Christ.

We know that many today view Africa as a poor and marginalized continent. The question for the church in Africa, however, is not, "How do others see us?" The question is, "How do we see ourselves?" At Azusa the people saw themselves not as poor and powerless, but as people of eternal destiny. They saw themselves as God's last-days messengers, empowered by His Spirit to take the good news to the nations before Christ's soon coming. They truly believed that by being baptized in the Holy Spirit they had received the power they needed to get the job done.

Like William Seymour and the believers at Azusa, we, the Pentecostal church in Africa must also see ourselves as people of destiny. Truly, Africa's time has come. God is now calling Africa to great missions endeavor. Just as one hundred years ago the gospel went powerfully from Azusa Street to Africa, today it must go powerfully from Africa to the nations.

The Heart of True Pentecostalism

Secondly, the Azusa Street Outpouring reminds us that missions is at the heart of true Pentecostalism. Jesus clearly placed it there (Acts 1:8). In the same way, the Azusa Street Revival had its focus on all the nations of the world. During the first three years of the revival dozens of missionaries went out from that small mission to many parts of the world. In addition, scores of missionaries and missionary movements were inspired by the outpouring.

Azusa reminds us that any form of Pentecostalism that does not place missions at its center is not true Pentecostalism. Early twentieth-century Pentecostal missiology was characterized by three burning beliefs: (1) that Jesus was coming soon, (2) that the lost in all nations must be reached before He comes again, (3) and that God was pouring out His Spirit in the last days to empower the church for the task. The combining of these beliefs produced a powerful missionary synergy. The baptism in the Holy Spirit provided the necessary power and boldness to attempt the work. Pentecostal historian Gary B. McGee notes that "the overriding ethos of Pentecostalism" both then and now is "the urgency to evangelize the world ahead of the imminent return of Jesus Christ."[1]

J. Roswell Flower, an early leader in the Assemblies of God, was baptized in the Holy Spirit in 1908, during the height of the Azusa Street Revival. In that same year he wrote,

> The baptism of the Holy Ghost does not consist in simply speaking in tongues. No. It has a much more grand and a deeper meaning than that. It fills our souls with the love of God for lost humanity, and makes us much more willing to leave home, friends, and all to work in His vineyard, even if it be far away among the heathen. . . . "Go ye into all the world and preach the gospel to every creature." This command of Jesus can only be properly fulfilled

---

[1]Gary B. McGee, "Regions Beyond," 69.

68

when we have obeyed that other command, "Tarry
ye in the city of Jerusalem till ye be endued with
power from on high." When we have tarried and
received that power, then, and then only are we fit
to carry the gospel. When the Holy Spirit comes
into our hearts, the missionary spirit comes with it;
they are inseparable, as the missionary spirit is but
one of the fruits of the Holy Spirit. Carrying the
gospel to hungry souls in this and other lands is but
a natural result of receiving the baptism in the Holy
Ghost.[2]

These early Pentecostal missionaries became, in the words of
Vinson Synan, "missionaries of the one way ticket."[3] By this Synan
meant that many of these missionaries, once they left for the field,
never intended to return to the land of their birth. They had
decided to forsake all to take the good news of Jesus to the
unreached people of Africa and other parts of the world. God is
now calling the Assemblies of God in Africa to be a shining light
unto the nations. In preparation for that task the leadership of the
church is calling out to God for a new continent-wide Pentecostal
outpouring.

---

[2]J. Roswell Flower, Editorial, *The Pentecost* (August 1908), 4, in Gary B. McGee,
This Gospel Shall Be Preached, vol. 1, (Springfield, MO: Gospel Publishing
House, 1986), 45-46.

[3]Vinson Synan, *The Spirit Said 'Grow'* (Monrovia, CA: MARC Publications,
1992), 39.

The Purpose and Necessity of Spirit Baptism.

We also learn from the Azusa Revival the purpose and necessity of Spirit baptism. The leaders of the Azusa Street Revival clearly understood both. They understood its purpose to be empowerment for last-days witness. Seymour wrote in the first edition of *The Apostolic Faith*, "This is a world-wide revival, the last Pentecostal revival to bring our Jesus."[4] In the second edition he wrote, "We expect to see a wave of salvation go over this world."[5]

The primary purpose of Spirit-baptism is empowerment for global witness. Jesus said, "You will receive power when the Holy Spirit comes on you; and you will be my witnesses in Jerusalem, and in all Judea and Samaria, and to the ends of the earth" (Acts 1:8). As Africa calls upon God for a new Pentecost, it must be ever mindful of the global purpose of the experience. Tragically, too many Pentecostal churches in Africa today are in danger of becoming side-tracked onto less important issues. Rather than focusing on reaching the lost, many are focusing on wealth, prosperity, and personal blessing. While many personal blessings come from being filled with the Spirit, we must never forget that the primary calling of the Pentecostal church in Africa—as it is anywhere else in the world—is the evangelization of the nations. Further, the primary purpose of the Pentecostal experience is empowerment for such witness.

---

[4]*The Apostolic Faith,* September 1906, 4.
[5]*The Apostolic Faith,* October 1906, 1.

The leaders of the Azusa Street Revival also understood the necessity of Spirit baptism. They believed that because every Christian was called to be a witness; therefore, every Christian needed to be personally empowered by the Spirit. This belief motivated them to proclaim Pentecost far and wide. Their zeal for Pentecost is reflected in what was possibly the favorite song at Azusa, "The Comforter Has Come":

> *O spread the tidings 'round,*
> *Wherever man is found,*
> *Wherever human hearts*
> *And human woes abound.*
> *Let every Christian tongue*
> *Proclaim the joyful sound,*
> *The Comforter has come!*

As more and more believers were empowered by the Spirit, the movement picked up momentum and spread around the world. As Africa prepares to take the message of Christ to the nations, the church must ensure that every believer is empowered by the Spirit.

Tremendous Potential

Finally, from the Azusa Street Revival we learn something about Africa's tremendous potential. The African church, like those early Pentecostals at Azusa, has the potential of success far beyond its grandest dreams. The participants in the Azusa Street could never have imagined the far-reaching impact of what was happening in their small mission in Los Angeles. They were simply following what they believed the Spirit was telling them to do. One hundred years later, we know the profound affect that revival has had on the world. Today, there are more than 500 million Pentecostals meeting in over a million local churches around the world. During the twentieth century Pentecostalism has grown to be one of the most powerful missionary movements in the history of the church.

At the Second General Council of the newly-formed Assemblies of God (AG) in September, 1914, about 500 Pentecostal pastors and missionaries met in Chicago, Illinois. There they passed a resolution dedicating themselves and the movement to the greatest evangelism in the history of the church. Today the AG counts over 50 million adherents in 280 thousand churches in 212 countries and territories around the world. In Africa and the Indian Ocean Basin the AG has over 13 million members in 34 thousand churches in 44 countries. There is now an emerging missionary movement among the African Assemblies of God churches across the continent with national, regional, and continental missions boards being organized to coordinate the effort. The Assemblies of God in Africa is mobilizing for world missions!

And yet, much remains to be done. The task of closure (i.e., taking the gospel to every tribe, tongue, nation, and people) remains before the church. According to the Joshua Project there remain 2.5 billion unreached people in the world today. These people represent 39.5% of the world's population and live in 6,899 unreached people groups.[6] No longer can the church depend on one segment (the western church) to carry the torch of missions to the nations. It is—as it has always been—the task of the entire body of Christ. The gospel must go from all nations to all nations.

And no longer can the church be content to go about the business of missions in its own ability, neglecting the empowering work of the Holy Spirit. Now is the time to call on God for a new Pentecost to empower the Church to complete the Great Commission in this decade!

How great is Africa's potential! If the Assemblies of God in Africa were to experience a powerful new Pentecostal outpouring, with millions of its members being baptized in the Holy Spirit, only heaven can tell what its profound impact on the nations could be. As thousands of Spirit-empowered African missionaries go from Africa to the nations, multiplied millions could be swept into the kingdom of God, and entire yet-to-be-reached people groups could turn to Christ. May it be so, O, Lord!

The African church has committed itself to doing its part in fulfilling the Great Commission of Christ. It can take inspiration from those early Pentecostals at Azusa Street. If God used them to impact the nations, then He can use Africa too! All that remains is that Africa experience a new Pentecost, and then fully follow Christ's command to preach the gospel in power in all the world.

---

[6] Joshua Project Website. Available <http://www.joshuaproject.net/global statistics.php> (4 October 2005).

CHAPTER 8

OH LORD, DO IT AGAIN!

I once read the story of an old Salvation Army soldier who stood at the grave side of General William Booth, founder of the Salvation Army. As he pondered the powerful influence of Booth's life, he prayed, "Oh, Lord, Do it again!" As we ponder the global impact of the Azusa Street Revival and the worldwide missionary movement it birthed, we also cry out to God, "Oh, Lord! Do it again." Send a similar outpouring to the church in Africa. Prepare the African church for its God-ordained destiny. If the church in Africa is to rise up and be all that God intends it to be, it must, like the first-century church, "stay in the city until [it has] been clothed with power from on high" (Luke 24:49).

Africa is Ready

All indicators point to the fact that the church in Africa is ready for a new twenty-first century Pentecostal outpouring. One indicator is the growing awareness among church leaders of the church's need. As Africa mobilizes for mission, national leaders across the continent are calling their churches back to their Pentecost roots. In the year 2000 the leadership of the Africa Assemblies of God Alliance put out a call to the AG in Africa to go "Back to the Upper Room." God delights in those who are prepared to do His will, and He stands ready to fill and empower all who are prepared to preach His gospel to the nations.

My own experience also indicates that Africa is ready for a new Pentecostal outpouring. It has been my privilege during the past ten years to travel throughout Africa teaching and preaching in Eleventh Hour Institutes and Holy Spirit Empowerment Conferences. I have ministered in seventeen countries in every region of Africa preaching and teaching on the baptism in the Holy Spirit and related issues. I have seen many thousands of Africans gloriously baptized in the Holy Spirit and speaking in tongues as the Spirit enabled.

It is my considered opinion that Africa is ready for a new Pentecost. There is in the hearts of Africans a deep hunger for God. And there is a strong desire to get involved in the global mission of God, along with a readiness to receive His empowering for the job.

The Spirit of God is speaking to the African church in a new and compelling way. The Spirit is saying to the church, "Now is Africa's time." We must therefore seize the moment. Our prayer must be, "Oh Lord, do it again! Pour out your Spirit upon us just as you did at Pentecost—and just as you did at Azusa."

An important postscript: Throughout this book we have talked much about an experience called the baptism in the Holy Spirit. We have described it as a wonderful life-changing experience that empowers one for Christian witness. You may be asking, "How can I receive this wonderful experience?" Included in this book are two appendices. Appendix 1 answers the question, "What must I do to be saved?" (Salvation is a necessary prerequisite for Spirit baptism.) Appendix 2 answers the question, "How may I be baptized in the Holy Spirit?" If you are hungry to experience God's presence and power in your life, read these two articles, and follow the instructions in them. You too can be empowered by God's Spirit today!

APPENDIX 1

How to Be Saved

Before one can be baptized in the Holy Spirit he or she must first be born again (John 3:1-7).[1] Jesus said that the world—that is, those who do not know Christ—cannot receive the Holy Spirit (John 14:17). Peter told the crowd on the Day of Pentecost that they must first repent and be baptized before they could receive the gift of the Holy Spirit (Acts 2:38).

You ask, "How then can I be saved and come to know Christ as my own personal Savior?" The Bible teaches that to be saved you must first realize your need for salvation (Rom. 3:23). You must be willing to admit that you are a sinner and that you stand condemned before a holy God (John 3:18). You must also understand that, in Christ, God has made the way for you to be saved (Isa. 53:6; 2 Cor. 5:21). Jesus died in your place on the cross that you might be brought back to God (Rom. 5:10).

Once you understand these things, you must be willing to come to Christ in repentance and faith (Acts 20:21; Heb. 6:1). You begin by repenting of your sins. You do this by praying and admitting to God that you are a sinner (1 John 1:8-10), and by

---

[1] As you read, you should take your Bible and carefully read all of the Scripture passages indicated.

asking God to forgive you of your sins. You must then turn from those sins to live a life pleasing to God (2 Tim. 2:19).

Though repentance is essential, it, in itself, is not enough. You must now turn to Christ and put your faith in Him alone for salvation (Acts 4:12; 16:31). You must believe that Christ died in your place for your sins on the cross, and that He rose again on the third day (Rom. 10:9-10). Then, by faith, invite Him into your life as Lord and Savior (Rev. 3:20). If you are prepared to do these things, pray this prayer from your heart:

> "Lord Jesus, I admit that I am a sinner and stand condemned before a holy God. I believe that You died on the cross for my sins, and that God raised You from the dead on the third day. Jesus, I put my trust in You alone for salvation. Forgive me of my sins, come into my heart, and be my Lord and Savior. I now turn from my sins to follow You all the days of my life. In Your name I pray. Amen."

If you have sincerely prayed this prayer, then you have been born anew (2 Cor. 5:17). You have been made ready for heaven. But much more, you have been made ready to serve God while on your way to heaven. You must now follow Christ with all your heart (Matt. 16:24). You can do this by finding a good Spirit-filled church with a pastor who faithfully preaches the word of God. Join that church, be baptized in water, read your Bible, and pray every day.

Also realize that there are other people like you who need to know Christ as their Savior. God will give you His Holy Spirit to empower you to reach those people for Him (Acts 1:8). You can learn how to receive the power of the Spirit by reading Appendix 2, "How to Be Filled with the Holy Spirit."

APPENDIX 2

How to Be Filled with the Spirit

Throughout this book we have talked about the baptism in the Holy Spirit.[1] We have described Spirit baptism as a powerful life-altering experience from God. With the experience many blessings come into the Christian's life. The primary purpose of Spirit baptism, however, is empowerment for witness.

We will now answer the question, "How can one personally receive this powerful experience into his or her own life? In answering this question we will discuss three important issues: preparing to receive the Spirit, receiving the Spirit, and speaking in tongues.

Preparing to Receive the Spirit

Before one can receive Spirit baptism he must prepare himself (or herself) to receive. There are three prerequisites for receiving the Spirit: First, one must be truly born again. The baptism in the Holy Spirit is a gift that the Father gives only to His children (Luke 11 9-13). If you are not sure of your salvation, go back and read Appendix 1, "How to Be Saved."

---

[1]To be baptized in the Holy Spirit and to be filled with the Spirit describe the same experience (Acts 1:5; cf. 2:4). They are two of many phrases used in the New Testament to describe the same experience.

Secondly, before one can be filled with the Spirit he must hunger and thirst after God. Jesus said, "Blessed are those who hunger and thirst for righteousness, for they will be filled" (Matt. 5:6). On another occasion Jesus cried out, "If anyone is thirsty, let him come to me and drink. Whoever believes in me, as the Scripture has said, streams of living water will flow from within him" (John 7:37-38). He was speaking about the Holy Spirit (v. 39). Are you thirsty for more of God? Do you long to live closer to Him and be of greater service to Him and His kingdom? If your answer to these questions is yes, then you can be filled with His Spirit today!

Finally, to receive the Spirit one must be committed

obeying God's command to be His witness (Acts 1:4-8). The Bible says, that God gives the Holy Spirit "to those who obey Him" (Acts 5:32). If you are prepared to obey God, God is prepared to give you His Holy Spirit.

Receiving the Spirit

Like salvation, Spirit-baptism is received by faith (Gal. 3:14).[2] Jesus said that the Holy Spirit flows through those who believe (John 7:37-38). As you come to Jesus to receive the baptism in the Holy Spirit, believe that He will give it to you. He has promised that He will (Luke 11:13). There are three "faith steps" that you can take in receiving the Holy Spirit:

---

[2] It will be very profitable if you look up all of the verses referenced in this chapter.

1. First, you ask in faith. Speaking of the Holy Spirit, Jesus said, "Ask, and it will be given to you . . ." (Luke 11:9). Pray this prayer:

> "Jesus, You promised. You said that if I would ask, You would give me the Holy Spirit. You said that everyone who asks receives. So, I ask You right now, give me the Holy Spirit; fill me and empower me to be Your witness. Amen."

As you pray, believe that God is hearing your prayer, and that, at this very moment, He is answering your prayer and filling you with His Spirit. Focus your attention on what God is doing for and in you. You will begin to sense the Spirit's presence as He comes upon you.

2. Now, receive by faith. Receiving the Spirit is a definite act of faith. It occurs at a definite point in time when the gift of the Holy Spirit is fully received. It can be compared to Peter's step of faith when he, at the command of Jesus, stepped from the boat and began to walk on water (Matt. 14:29).

Jesus not only instructed us to ask for the Holy Spirit (Luke 11:9-13), He also told us how we are to ask: "Therefore I say to you, all things for which you pray and ask, believe that you have received them, and they will be granted you" (Mark 11:24). Notice that Jesus did not say, "believe that you will receive." He said "believe that you have received." This faith is not a passive or future-oriented faith. It is rather an active faith, located in the immediate present. The act of receiving the Spirit is a bold present-tense step of faith.

At this point pray with complete confidence in the promises of Christ. Say and believe, "I truly believe that I have received the Holy Spirit!" In response to your act of faith, the Holy Spirit will fill you with His power and presence. If you will remain sensitive to what God is doing, deep within your spirit you will sense the Spirit's coming and filling you.

3. It is now time for you to speak in faith. All that remains for you to do at this point is to speak out in faith. On the Day of Pentecost the 120 disciples "were all filled with the Holy Spirit and began to speak . . ." (Acts 2:4). As they spoke, the Spirit flowed into, through, and out of them. They "began to speak with other tongues, as the Spirit was giving them utterance." When you are filled with the Spirit, you too should expect to speak in tongues.

Speaking in Tongues

You should know, however, that the words you speak will not come from your mind, as in natural speech, but from deep inside, from your spirit. Jesus said, "He who believes in Me, as the Scripture said, 'From his innermost being will flow rivers of living water'" (John 7:38). Speaking in tongues is not an activity of the human mind but of the human spirit. It is not a mental but a spiritual exercise. It proceeds from one's innermost being. Paul wrote, "For one who speaks in a tongue does not speak to men but to God; for no one understands, but in his spirit he speaks mysteries" (1 Cor. 14:2). Paul further stated, "For if I pray in a tongue, my spirit prays, but my mind is unfruitful" (v. 14).

When you come to God to be filled with the Spirit, you should relax and open your heart fully to Him. Then, in faith ask for the Holy Spirit, fully expecting God to answer your prayer. As you wait on God, sense the presence of the Spirit coming upon you. Then, through a conscious act of faith, "believe that you have received." You will sense the Spirit's powerful presence deep within, filling and empowering you. By this you will know that God is indeed filling you with the Holy Spirit! You must, now act in bold faith and begin to speak from the Presence, that is, from where you sense God's Spirit deep within.

Your speaking will not be a forced effort, but a natural flow of supernatural words. You should simply allow it to happen, and cooperate fully with the Spirit by boldly speaking out in faith. You will begin to speak words you do not understand, words that are coming from the Spirit of God. When this happens, don't be afraid. Just let the words flow!

Although no two peoples' Spirit baptisms are exactly the same, everyone can expect certain things to happen. The first, as mentioned above, you can expect to speak in tongues as the Spirit enables (Acts 2:4; 10:44-46; 19:6). Secondly, you will receive zeal and boldness to share Christ with others (Acts 2:14, 4:31). Further, you can expect a greater awareness of the Spirit's presence in your life, a greater liberty in worship and prayer (2 Cor. 3:17; Eph. 5:18-20), and an increased flow of the Spirit, resulting in more effective ministry (John 7:37-38).

A Final Word

You should not make the mistake that many have made. Do not think that once you have been baptized in the Spirit, you have somehow "arrived," and there is nothing more you need to do in order to maintain a Spirit-empowered life. Spirit baptism will bring you into a new and deeper relationship with God. That relationship, however, must be continually renewed. No matter how powerful your initial infilling may be, if the experience does not find further expression in a life of sincere devotion, disciplined prayer, holiness, and committed witness, the power of the experience will soon fade.

Bibliography

Alexander, Estrelda Alexander, *The Women of Azusa Street*. Laurel, MD: The Seymour Press, 2012.

Bartleman, Frank. *Azusa Street*. South Plainfield, NJ: Bridge Publishing, Inc., 1980.

Ewart, Frank. *The Phenomenon of Pentecost*. Hazelwood, MO: World Aflame Press, 1947.

Flower, J. Roswell. "Editorial," *The Pentecost*. August 1908.

Frodsham, Stanley H. *With Signs Following: The Story of the Later-Day Pentecostal Revival*, Springfield, MO: Gospel Publishing House, 1946. In *The Globalization of Pentecostalism: A Religion Made to Travel*, eds., Murray A. Dempster, Byron D. Klaus and Douglas Petersen. Oxford, UK: Regnum Books International, 1999.

Goss, Ethel. *Winds of God*. New York: Cornet Press Books, 1958

Joshua Project website. http://www.joshuaproject.net/ globalstatistics.php. Accessed October 4, 2005.

Lake, John G. *Adventures in God*. Tulsa, OK: Harrison House Publishers, 1981.

_____. "Origin of *The Apostolic Faith* Movement," in *The Pentecostal Outlook*, September 1932. In Larry Martin. *The Life and Ministry of William J. Seymour*. Joplin, MO: Christian Life Books, 1999.

_____. "Spiritual Hunger," in *John G. Lake: The Complete Collection of His Life Teachings*, ed. Roberts Liardon. Tulsa, OK: Albury Publishing, 1999.

Liardon, Roberts. *The Azusa Revival.* Shippensburg, PA: Destin Image Publishers, 2006.

Lindsay, Gordon, ed. *John G. Lake: Apostle to Africa.* Dallas, TX: Christ for the Nations, 1979.

McGee, Gary B. "Missions, Overseas (North American)," *Dictionary of Pentecostal and Charismatic Movements.* Eds. Stanley M. Burgess and Gary B. McGee. Grand Rapids, MI: Regency Reference Library, Zondervan Publishing House, 1988.

_____. *This Gospel Shall Be Preached*, Vol. 1. Springfield, MO: Gospel Publishing House, 1986.

_____. "To the Regions Beyond: The Global Expansion of Pentecostalism" in *The Century of the Holy Spirit: 100 Years of Pentecostal and Charismatic Renewal.* Ed., Vinson Synan. Nashville, TN: Thomas Nelson, Inc., 2001.

Owens, Robert. "The Azusa Street Revival: The Pentecostal Movement Begins in America." in *The Century of the Holy Spirit: 100 Years of Pentecostal and Charismatic Renewal.* Ed., Vinson Synan. Nashville, TN: Thomas Nelson, Inc., 2001.

Sizelove, Rachel, "A Sparkling Fountain for the Whole Earth." *Word and Work,* Vol. 56, No. 6 (June 1934), 2.

_____. "A Sketch of My Life," unpublished manuscript.

Synan, Vinson. *The Spirit Said 'Grow'.* Monrovia, CA: MARC Publications, 1992.

The Apostolic Faith. Los Angeles California, 1906-1909.

Other Decade of Pentecost Books

Order from ActsinAfrica@agmd.org

*Proclaiming Pentecost: 100 Sermons Outlines on the Power
of the Holy Spirit* (2011), Associate editor with
Mark Turney, editor (Also available in French,
Spanish, Portuguese, and Swahili)

Globalizing Pentecostal Missions in Africa (2011)
Editor, with Enson Lwesya
(Also available in French, 2014)

*Power for Mission: The Africa Assemblies of God
Mobilizing the Reach the Nations* (2014)
Editor, with Enson Lwesya

Other Books by Denzil R. Miller

Available at www.DenzilRMiller.com

Power Ministry: How to Minister in the Spirit's Power (2004)
(Also available in French, Portuguese, Kiswahili,
Malagasy, Kinyarwanda, and Chichewa)

*Empowered for Global Mission: A Missionary Look
at the Book of Acts* (2005)

From Azusa to Africa to the Nations (2005)
(Also available in French, Spanish, and Portuguese)

Acts: The Spirit of God in Mission (2007)

*In Step with the Spirit: Studies in the
Spirit-filled Walk* (2008)

*The Kingdom and the Power: The Kingdom of God:
A Pentecostal Interpretation* (2009)

*Experiencing the Spirit: A Study of the Work of
the Spirit in the Life of the Believer* (2009)

Teaching in the Spirit (2009)

*Power Encounter: Ministering in the Power and
Anointing of the Holy Spirit: Revised* (2009)
(Also available in Kiswahili)

*You Can Minister in God's Power: A Guide for
Spirit-filled Disciples* (2009)

*The Spirit of God in Mission: A Vocational
Commentary on the Book of Acts* (2011)

Proclaiming Pentecost: 100 Sermon Outlines on the Power of the Holy Spirit (2011), Associate editor with Mark Turney, editor (Also available in French, Spanish, Portuguese, and Swahili)

Globalizing Pentecostal Missions in Africa (2011) Editor, with Enson Lwesya (Also available in French, 2014)

The 1:8 Promise of Jesus: The Key to World Harvest (2012)

Power for Mission: The Africa Assemblies of God Mobilizing the Reach the Nations (2014) Editor, with Enson Lwesya

Missionary Tongues Revisited: More than an Evidence: Recapturing Luke's Missional Perspective on Speaking in Tongues (2014)

NOTES

NOTES

NOTES

NOTES

NOTES

www.ingramcontent.com/pod-product-compliance
Lightning Source LLC
Chambersburg PA
CBHW060125050426
42448CB00010B/2025